# BUDDHIST

© 1988 Franklin Watts
This edition 1997

Franklin Watts
96 Leonard Street
London EC2A 4RH

Franklin Watts Australia
14 Mars Road
Lane Cove
NSW 2066

ISBN: 0 86313 674 5 (hardback)
ISBN: 0 7496 2267 9 (paperback)

Design: Edward Kinsey

Typesetting: Tradespools Ltd

Printed by G. Canale, Turin, Italy

The publishers would like to thank
the Samarasekara family and all the
people shown in this book.

Ven. Dr. H. Saddhatissa is Head
Monk at the London Buddhist
Vihara in Chiswick, West London

Note: Many of the photographs in
this book originally appeared
in 'My Belief: I am a Buddhist'

# BUDDHIST

Jenny Wood

Photographs: Chris Fairclough

Consultant: Ven. Dr. H. Saddhatissa

**Watts Books**
London/New York/Sydney

This family are Buddhists.
They follow the teachings
and way of life of the Buddha.

The Buddha was a prince
who lived in ancient India.
He went in search of wisdom.

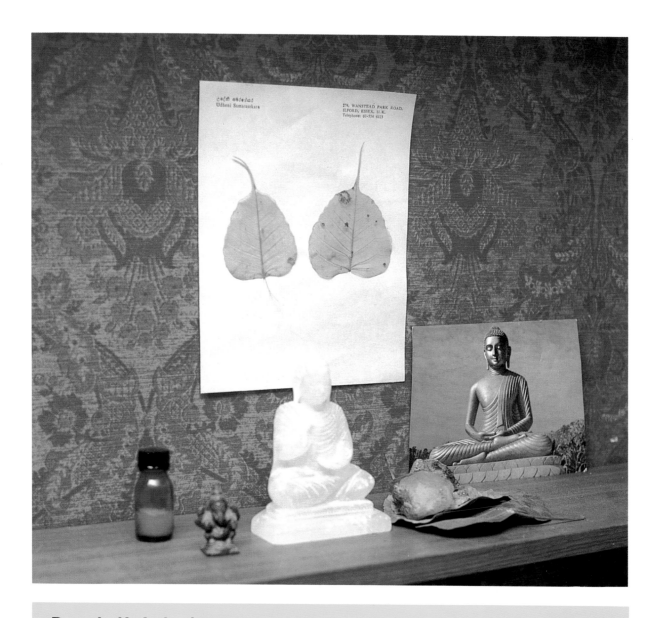

Buddhists keep many things
in their home to remind them
of the Buddha's teachings.

There is no special Buddhist dress
for everyday wear.
Women usually wear the dress
of the country from which they come.
This family come from Sri Lanka.

Buddhist men in Britain
usually wear European clothes.
A woman's sari is one piece of cloth
up to six metres long.

On days when there is a full moon,
special ceremonies are held.
Simple white clothes are worn.

A Buddhist temple
is called a Vihara.
Buddhists worship there
whenever they can.

Buddhists take off their shoes
before going into the Vihara.
They light candles in front of
a statue of the Buddha.

They also offer gifts
of flowers and food to the Buddha.
While they do this, they recite
special verses, called gathas.

One ceremony which takes place
at the Vihara before midday
almost every day is Dana,
the offering of food to the monks.

Buddhist monks have shaven heads.
They wear orange robes.
They do not eat after midday.

The monks chant verses
from the Holy Books,
and help people to understand
the teachings of the Buddha.

Many children attend Sunday School
at the Vihara to learn
about the life of the Buddha
and his teachings.

Buddhists can eat whatever they like.
Many choose not to eat
meat, fish or eggs.

Main meals often consist of
curried meat and vegetable dishes
with boiled rice.

A Buddhist wedding takes place
at home or in a hotel.
The bride and groom are led on to
a special platform
decorated with white flowers.

The bride and groom exchange rings.
The thumbs of their right hands
are tied together by
the bride's uncle.

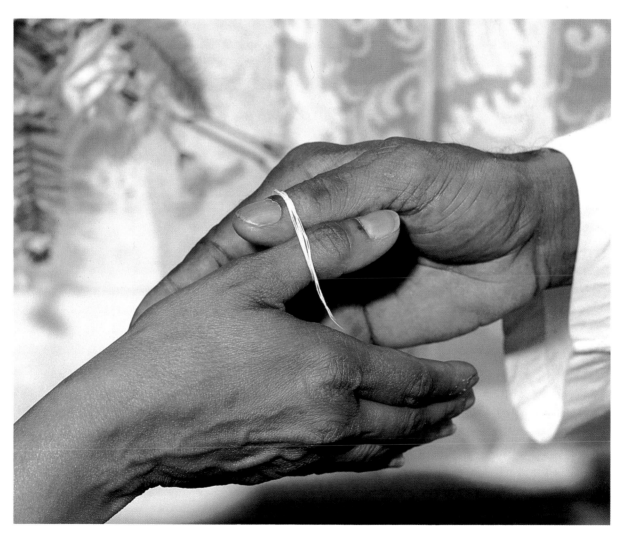

This family keep many things
to remind them of their homeland
and the Buddhist culture.

They celebrate the Buddhist festivals.
Brightly coloured masks
are sometimes worn.

Every day, Buddhist families
pray to the Buddha
and promise to live
according to his teachings.

# FACTS ABOUT BUDDHISTS

Prince Siddhartha Gautama, who became the Buddha, lived in India about 2,500 years ago. His thoughts and teachings are the basis of the Buddhist religion.

Buddhists do not think of the Buddha as a god, but as a great teacher.

Buddhists make promises to the Buddha every day. One of the most important of these is not to harm any living thing.

The Buddha taught his followers that they live many lives on this Earth until they become good enough to reach a state of perfect peace called Nirvana.

There are thought to be about 1,000 million Buddhists in the world today. They are found in nearly every country.

About 60,000 Buddhists live in Great Britain. Most of them came originally from Sri Lanka, India, China, Burma or Tibet.

# GLOSSARY

**Buddha**
The name given to Prince Siddhartha Gautama, the founder of the Buddhist religion.

**Dana**
The ceremony of offering food to the monks in the Vihara.

**Full-moon day**
The Buddhist holy day, each month, on which special events are celebrated.

**Gathas**
Verses which are recited during worship.

**Monk**
A man who is a member of a religious community. Buddhist monks have shaven heads and wear orange robes.

**Sari**
A dress made from one piece of cloth wound round the body. The piece of cloth can be up to six metres long.

**Vihara**
A Buddhist temple.

# INDEX